AS A MAN
CHOOSES

RANDALL CORELLI

EXULON
ELITE

CONTENTS

INTRODUCTION

For centuries, people have been seeking the truth about reality; their reality, their lives. The major religions of the world have attempted to provide the answers. Their answers are often compelling, well meaning, and provide helpful (and necessary) guidance for life's challenges. However, when it comes down to having a truly successful life, "helpful" just doesn't get it done. Add in some unintended misdirection, myth, and downright falsehood, and you have a diluted solution at best.

This book was written to give you the best shot at a successful life.

This book is a short, compact, and powerful piece of motivational dynamite, wisdom and revelation that becomes the supercharger on your entire life. No wasted words here, just straight talk compiled over half a century of life experience, a life filled with too much adversity to write down in one volume.

So you get the concentrate, minus the pain, disappointment, and travail that went into learning all that is here. It's what I wish I knew from the start, from day one. Did you ever wish you could live your life over, looking back at all the wrong choices you have made, vowing how it would be different a second time around? *Well, think of this book as a new beginning, as a virtual second time around.*

Do you have children? Young adults and even teenagers may find this to be the advantage that surpasses all others. When these truths become part of your teenager's very nature and being, the heritage that is left behind with them is a *powerful set of habits and beliefs* that extend beyond the very circumstances, misfortunes, or adversities that we all experience. In effect, they grow up driving tanks through life's difficulties when others are being driven off the road in their bicycles, scooters, and compact cars. It's been said by some that life should come with a handbook, instruction guide or manual (it's also been said about children).

Well, think of this book as your "Life 101" handbook. I have to warn you, though, because once you have been exposed to the truth about your reality, you will be out of excuses.

A life lived without excuses is a powerful life indeed!

All the best,

Randall Corelli

DEDICATION

To my beautiful wife Teresa, the best choice I ever made.

As a Man Chooses

Man, the master of his fate and destiny, is unaware of the power given to him by the Creator. He looks to the divine to magically solve all his problems, bless him with all the desires of his heart, and provide a heaven on earth. Not finding the answers, he looks toward any one of a thousand purveyors of success and happiness, and they also disappoint, sometimes in spectacular ways. Now, almost without hope and at the end of his rope, man will reach out to fortune tellers, drugs, alcohol, or anyone of a hundred addictions that offer some hope or mind-numbing distraction to depression, anxiety, and despair. In the end, man reaches out to the government to shield him from the total disaster that is now his life. The government, all too happy to gain control and power over the people, consolidates its hold on man's impoverished state and relegates him to a subsistence life that hangs in the balance day by day.

Surely, it has not come to this, or has it?

How different it would be if from an early age, man was taught the most basic and powerful of all human truths? *A man's life is no more than a compilation of the accumulated choices he has made since birth.* Literally, figuratively and every other way, as a man chooses, so shall his life be. This fundamental law and truth in life is so basic and inexorably true that it's all but lost on the vast majority, saved for the most grounded and wise men. There can be no other law so powerful and unyielding as this anchor of human existence, and it works for you or against you, day after day, week after week, year after year.

So, let's examine how this bedrock of life and all powerful force of God's Divine plan for man can and will play out in each major area of your life.

OVERALL STATE OF BEING

A man, by design, is programed to seek out that which he perceives will bring him happiness, a blessed state of overall well being. God has provided man with an opportunity to be in relationship with Him, to know Him through His word, and be led by Him through His Holy Spirit. Men that choose to invest a steady portion of their time, energy, strength, and will in God, choosing to act on His revelations, experience the *fruit of the spirit*. The fruit of the spirit is love, joy, peace, forbearance, kindness, goodness, gentleness, and self-control. Thus man, by rightly choosing God, experiences a steady stream of happiness that cannot but be temporarily altered by life's uncertainties. Men that avoid God, His word, and His Spirit find themselves in an unpredictable state of human passions, emotions, and feelings that resemble a roller coaster at an amusement park. Up, down, sideways, and with no real stability, sanity, or purpose. Often faced with out of control circumstances and competitive worldly forces, this man then experiences anger, bitterness, lust, hate, fear, and the like. His overall state is anything but blessed, and he consoles himself with the brief moments when all is right (or appears to be). Should life take an unexpected twist or sharp wrong turn, he has no foundation to right his internal gyroscope and is then hopelessly lost, maybe forever. Clearly, choosing God is the master choice affecting all other choices, an absolute necessity for a man desiring an optimal life.

THOUGHT

Each man has thousands and thousands of thoughts every day, and there can be no avoiding the imprint on him, his circumstances and his overall well being. Second only to rightful relationship with God, a man's choice of thoughts, dwellings, plans, and machinations are similar to a construction site that is continuously a work in progress. The building and edifice that the architect has in mind has a good chance of becoming his reality, as long as the construction stays focused and true to the design and plan.

A mind that has no plan or no governing set of right or wrong will create a progressively more tangled mess until the edifice of their life is of little to no value. Rightful thinking is the engine behind all purposeful action.

So what constitutes rightful thinking? *A man that chooses to focus on his blessings and his opportunities in life finds himself grateful and thankful for all the Creator has bestowed on him.* The very center of his being is full of light and peace and there is a general feeling of good things to come. This optimism encourages forgiveness, trust, love and confidence.

Forgiveness, the act of letting go of an offense, makes room for mistakes and there is an acceptance of others that expands one's circle and arc of influence.

Non-judgment opens up the way for unconditional love, so a steady stream of goodness and kindness is regularly directed toward one's neighbor. This furthers confidence, as there is no hidden stockpile of judgment or hate ready to double back on its originator.

As this grateful man reflects on his blessings, he has thoughts of *humility* and a sense of wonder at what other blessings or opportunities may be coming in the future. His humility programs his daily life, as he knows that he never arrives, needs the cooperation of his friend and coworker, and takes nothing for granted. It also engenders loyalty, patience and love for those that have sown into his life, especially his Creator.

Finally, the thankful man reinvests his blessings in his family, his friends and his community. Wrong thinking, on the other hand, is a choice and is not a result of circumstance, birth, or genetics. Angry, disappointed or envious thoughts follow a focus on what has not gone right, followed by an impatient view of the future and what may be required. This man finds a way to *dwell* on what has gone wrong instead of what has gone right. These disappointments or failures loom large, like a giant skyscraper or apartment building, and they cast a shadow over every part of his existence. In effect, there is no sunshine, ever, and there is a sense of victimization, powerlessness, and an evil foreboding that the past may reappear at any moment. This generates feelings of fear, anxiety, worry, and even desperation. Opportunities shrink down to impossible long shots, and there is no patience where there is no faith or belief in a positive outcome. The spiral continues down with thoughts of inferiority, hate, jealousy, paranoia, self-centeredness, and self- absorption.

He now finds himself painted into the tightest possible corner, with no visible way out. The resulting desperation leads to gambling, drugs, alcohol abuse, crime, ill health and disability. Continued for extended periods of time, mental illness is a virtual certainty.

Can the man that has persisted in wrong thinking ever turn the corner and go down the right path? Maybe. If he is willing to change his thinking, consider the benevolence of his Creator, and choose to *reframe* his life. This reframing will certainly change his perspective and maybe his heart. From out of the heart springs the thoughts and words that define his destiny.

FRIENDS AND ASSOCIATIONS

As a man chooses his friends, associates, and business
partners, so shall his very being become aligned
with their thoughts, values, goals, and aspirations. Day in
and day out, like a steady stream running through the
highways and byways of his brain, friends and associates literally recreate a man's motivations, aspirations, hopes, dreams and moral structure. A man that
chooses high-minded, ethical, motivated associations
finds that he too is positively charged and excited about
life's possibilities. His efforts to improve increase and
there is a noticeable change in every aspect of his life.
Like a sailboat that travels with a steady breeze, the
total effort required is lessened considerably and all
that is required is a steady hand and a watchful eye.

Indeed, the term "smooth sailing" epitomizes his
life with the right friends and connections. Sadly, the
man that indiscriminately chooses his associations
finds trouble at every turn. His morals are eroded, his

peace of mind is gone and he gradually sinks, as the toll on his psyche and often his finances is debilitating and seemingly unfair. The very same sailboat with all the *identical* capabilities now struggles mightily as it gets pushed backward by heavy headwinds and cross-winds. This boat may yet get where it hopes to be going, but the damage done is significant and the time and energy required are multiplied many times over. There is no escaping the daily dose of one's closest companions. Given enough time, one's very being begins to look and act like that of the crowd in which he spends the most time.

SPEECH

Often ignored, misunderstood, and disrespected, a man's choice of his words is the *powerhouse* that drives the engine of his life. Speaking thousands of words a day, a wise man assembles a spiritual fortress of goodness, kindness, joy, peace, and blessing and prosperity when his words are edifying, uplifting, and merciful. His thankful, optimistic, and gracious words create a tidal wave of blessings that eventually envelops him and all that are sufficiently close to him. The man that ignorantly or willfully (it little matters which) speaks ill of all has little to no chance of sustaining any kind of positive force in his life. Should he be struggling in life, he will continue to struggle. If through some great external fortune he is temporarily on top, his time there is cut short, unlikely to ever rise again. *As a man chooses his words, so shall his life go.*

FOOD AND DRINK

Serving as the very *building blocks* of one's entire physical entity, food and drink are the inevitable purveyors of health and well being or disease, destruction, and disillusionment. *As a man chooses his form of nutrition or lack there of, so shall the very stability, longevity, health, well being, and stamina be decided.* Fresh, unadulterated whole food and drink, free of chemicals, excess sugars and additives are a virtual fountain of health, vitality and energy. This man exudes optimism, faith, and positive expectation. He is free of excess weight, upright, and without the body imbalances that would doom his metabolism.

Disease and sickness are unlikely events and they tend to move on rather quickly, being unwelcome visitors in such a robust environment. His less discriminating counterpart that opts for every manner of man-made, packaged, processed, and over-refined foodstuffs experiences a radically different destiny. He is plagued with excess weight, low energy, inefficient bodily functions and failing organs, constant disease, and resulting despair. Operating at less than half of his God-given capacity, this man falls woefully short of his potential, even if he should manage a brief period of prosperity and success. Should the man's extraordinary genetic background carry him a bit further, he still succumbs to premature aging and untimely death.

WIFE

Touching on virtually every aspect of a man's very existence, a wife has the *unique capacity* to create a bit of heaven on earth or hell on wheels for her mate. A woman with a good heart, a soft touch, and a gentle spirit is a source of continual blessing and favor to her husband. Generous, kind, patient and sensitive, this woman brings a balance and harmony to her marriage.

Conversely, a woman with a bad heart, unfeeling, and insensitive, is a destructive and competitive force in a marriage. Demanding, proud, and pushy, there is virtually no chance for balance, harmony, or peace.

While it is undeniably true that behind every successful man is often a good woman, but a bad woman with a mean or twisted spirit is a virtual tornado of destruction and despair. A wrong choice leads to alcoholism, drugs, crime, anger, and rage. There can be no more important choice than one of a spouse, and a wrong choice cries out for remedy at its earliest conve-

nience. *As a man chooses his wife, so will the very fabric of*

his existence be.

Finances

A man with sound financial management creates a continuous golden thread running through his life. Virtually every aspect of his existence, in some way, shape, or form, benefits from his work ethic and astute money management. Free of the stress of financial pressures, a man and his family are able to live and prosper in a way completely unknown and foreign to other men. Like a river running down hill, there is nothing that can successfully impede the blessing on all who know him. Prosperity leads to more prosperity, and the effect is such that a man's children and his children's children are blessed without any undue effort or strain on their part. It's as if they live in another world — insulated, protected and empowered to be all that the Creator has poured into their hearts and minds.

A man with erratic and unstable financial management and shaky work ethic finds himself continuously at odds with his wife, his family, and the world around him. It's as if the Creator himself has set his jaw against him, and there is no escape. Try though he might, this man cannot beg, borrow, steal, gamble, or connive his way out of his personal nightmare. All the would be short-term remedies lead to disaster in one way, shape or form.

Adding insult to injury, a man may try to live beyond his means and borrow his way to prosperity, only to find that he has sold his soul to the most unmerciful of all, the high-interest loan. His debt threatens his very existence as the payments all but insure that there is nothing left to grease the skids of everyday life. *As a man chooses his work ethic and money management techniques, so will the timber and tenor of his entire life look, sound, and feel.*

EDUCATION

As a man chooses his level of and commitment to education, so shall the ceiling on his life be.

A man that shuns education or minimizes its impact finds himself painted in a corner with no way out. Every way that he turns, he finds himself boxed in, frustrated, and unable to reach his goals and dreams. Should he possess extraordinary talent or be extremely gifted, it still leaves him with little width, breadth, and dimension to his life. If those gifts should ever fail him or become useless with age, he is now playing second fiddle to those that have invested in the business of educating themselves.

A man that values education, commits early to it, and stays with it creates an open door for his skills and talents. Should he find himself without a job, he can always try his hand at business or at teaching others. More often than not, the well-educated man that has managed to stay relevant finds opportunities and can make a good living and be a productive member of society.

If this same man dedicated himself to being one of the best in his field, he positions himself for extraordinary achievement and prosperity. Day in and day out, regardless of great economics or the lack thereof, the well-educated man lives in a broader, richer, and more diversified world than the man that opts out of the educational process. As he continues to educate and develop himself, the sky is the limit and life is never boring.

DREAMS AND GOALS

As a man chooses the goals and dreams for his life, so will the focus and emphasis of his very being reside.

Powerful goals, like strong movie stars and characters, create a vivid impression and lasting impact. Goals and dreams that are noble, noteworthy and broad-based will be edifying, inspiring, and beneficial to the man that has them. Motivation, energy, and drive flow freely as the excitement and purpose of these dreams propel him forward. Goals that are overly narrow, selfish, or one-dimensional are inherently dangerous and potentially self-destructive. More than one man has lost his family, health, and happiness and eventually his joy by exclusively pursuing financial success, power, and might.

A man that has no real dreams or goals is like a ship without a rudder, going wherever the current takes it on any particular day. At first the journey feels rather pleasant, and the man adrift may enjoy the sights, sounds and experiences usually reserved for the highly accomplished and independently wealthy. Without knowing it, this man has embraced the goal of hedonism and simply seeks to maximize his personal enjoyment and pleasure. As time goes by, he finds himself well downstream in life and the possibility of living a purposeful and possibly grand life get smaller and smaller. Should he remain adrift indefinitely, his life is literally and figuratively that of a bum: purpose-less, indulgent, and without character, substance, or achievement. In the end, it is as if he never lived at all, as there is no testimony or lasting tribute to his life on earth.

Physical Fitness

Man is, by the Creator's design, a complex physical entity, composed of bones, joints, organs, muscles, skin, tissue, etc. This amazing physical entity that is the physical man requires daily use and action to work properly, stay vital, and function effectively. For thousands of years, man was required to fully employ his physical capabilities to make a living, live, thrive, and survive. More often than not, man was strong, capable, and energetic until the very end of his life. Today's man has little in common with those of his forefathers. He has the privilege of living in a world of enormous technological power and might, and it simply displaces his desire and need for steady physical work and activity. He often works at a desk or drives a car or truck, and his free time mirrors his job as he is entertained, amused, and intrigued by the panorama of high-tech devices and appliances that eliminate the need to use his physical frame to enjoy himself. This man is in great danger of gradually losing his superb gift of strength, grace, and endurance.

As a man chooses his form, style, and frequency of fitness, so shall his physical being become transformed from barely functioning and alive to fully capable, strong, flexible, and able to endure most every kind of hardship.

Fitness that includes a variety of activities and motions see the most results, and the man that chooses the correct balance, stays strong and healthy well into old age.

ADVERSE CIRCUMSTANCES

The Creator made a perfect world, and to be in perfect relationship and harmony with him, but man chose another option. Rebellious by nature, man is isolated from God and His perfect love and blessings and experiences a variety of repercussions while on earth. Those repercussions take the form of adverse circumstances, and they can fall unevenly on men, sometimes dramatically and without apparent connection to a man's choices. Man then has to make the ultimate choice: how he reacts and acts in the face of sometimes overwhelming adversity, pain, and suffering. *As a man chooses his response to these trials, so shall his strength of character, will, and destiny be determined.*

A man that takes a longer-term view of life, both here and forever, sees the opportunity to build on his limited supply of resources and strength and calls on the Creator to empower him and his life for the maximum good and effectiveness. He reaches out to God, to others, and expands his circle of influence beyond the smaller world he lived in before the onset of adversity. He becomes a greater man than he was before, as he becomes part of the overall solution. Should he continue to experience adversity and persevere in his efforts to take on these challenges, he may become a true force for good and overpower the forces of evil that have attacked him. He is, as the saying goes, more than a conqueror.

A man that experiences adversity and chooses to shrink back from life finds himself in a whirlpool of despondency, despair and depression. His self focus increases and his inability to mount any effective counterattack against his situation leaves him an easy target to anxiety, depression, drugs, anger, crime, and the like. Instead of growing stronger through adversity, this man deteriorates at an ever-increasing rate if he cannot refocus himself on what is good and what he might do to remedy his situation. This man desperately needs to choose God, others, and a rededication to himself, his habits, and his hopes and dreams (even if they need to be altered).

COMMUNITY

Men live on a planet with other men, women and children and try as he might, cannot escape the reality of our interconnectedness and dependence on each other. *As a man chooses to acknowledge his brother, share his resources, and be kind and sympathetic to those in need, so shall his soul and spirit prosper and grow.* He is a force beyond his years and his goodness and kindness are a lasting testimony to his life on earth. This man cannot and will not be forgotten, and surely his Creator will acknowledge and remember him both in this life and the next.

A man that has no use for his neighbor, and cannot be bothered with his trials and tribulations, develops an increasingly narrow, shriveled, and dried up spirit. Holding tight to his possessions and offering little in the way of encouragement or hope, he isolates himself and leaves little opportunity to be known or know others that are outside of his immediate circle. More often than not, this man becomes increasingly judgmental, rigid, narrow and unavailable, certain that others are up to no good, out to get his money or take what is his. He is than an island unto himself and sure to be forgotten, unappreciated, and maybe even despised. His life ends when he dies and there is no future or hope, as he has chosen death instead of life, and thereby carries nothing forward into eternity with him.

TIME

*A*s a man chooses to use time, so shall his life progress, evolve and develop.

A man that has a full and complete understanding
of the value of time will move along an entirely different track than one that has no such understanding.
His days and nights are focused and there is no idle
chatter, indifferent work, or sloppy habits. Excess indul-
gence, addiction, and unneeded socializing or looking
for approval is not part of his daily life. Having an
understanding of the finite and limited amount of time
he has available, this man literally makes every minute
count so he experiences an ever-increasing return on
his life force. His life will often look like a parabola,
looking fairly modest in the beginning, but gradually
picking up speed until the cumulative results of all his
efforts suddenly rockets him forward in an upward
trajectory. At that point, this man rightly feels that he

has an almost unlimited future. Like the well known animated film star, it's to infinity and beyond.

The man that discounts time and sees it as ever-present and without end settles into an inefficient and unmotivated pattern of living. His days and nights are filled with endless distractions, compromises, and attempts to maximize his personal enjoyment and fun. Having a good time displaces his goals, dreams and aspirations — if he ever had any to begin with. Often, this man has developed a c'est la vie attitude and succumbs to the brainwashing that he can achieve his goals without any undue effort, hardship, or stress. Easy does it, that's his mantra, as he opens another beer or spends another three hours surfing the internet in a meaningless fashion. Technology alone will save him or so he thinks, and if not, well he can live at home until he is thirty-five and maybe get something going then. The cumulative effect of this wasteful use of time is a life that flat lines at best or gradually declines and then plummets at worst. Should he finally understand the enormous gift of time and decide to do something with it, he can start an upward trend that yields a rich harvest (if he does not settle back into his old ways). Even then, his potential has been reduced significantly and he may look back in awe at what could have been had he just lived a fully engaged and motivated life, thus maximizing his use of time.

COUNTRY AND STATE/PROVINCE

U nbeknownst to most men, he has a choice on where to reside and what country he can call home. With hundreds of countries to choose from, there are almost unlimited opportunities to find a suitable match for him and his family. Even within a country, there are widely varied lifestyles, morals, ideals, customs, and work opportunities as you travel from state to state or province to province.

As a man chooses his country and state/province, so shall he find opportunities for peace, happiness, joy and prosperity or the lack thereof.

A man that has taken the time to understand himself, his purpose, personality, hopes, dreams, and talents has positioned himself to choose the ideal locale. If he then decides to act on that knowledge, having sought advice from his Creator and wisest friends to corroborate his thinking, he often makes a transformative decision when he relocates.

Suddenly, what was frustrating, inhibiting, and maybe even disturbing about his life has totally vanished. He no longer struggles with the narrow thinking, prejudices, and sometimes belligerence and hostility that were dogging him in his old neighborhood. It's almost like the very gates of heaven have opened up and the immense liberation of an appropriate environment frees his mind, body, and soul to grow and prosper. As his life expands and his blessings become evident, his former relations, friends, and associates are beyond shocked at his progress. *It's almost impossible, they think, that this very same man is now such a star, when all we knew him he was a dud.* This man has literally reinvented himself or has been reinvented by his new location; it matters little. He is changed in a way that he probably never could have imagined.

The man that has no understanding or willingness to consider a location other than his current one cannot grow and prosper beyond the confines of the local traditions, laws, and restrictions of his current home. He is literally locked in place by the beliefs, opinions, and limitations of his original birthplace.

Should his current situation be a relatively happy one, he does well to stay put. A blessed and prosperous life is hard to come by, and the goodness of the current situation is in no way, shape, or form necessarily transferable to another homestead. In fact, more than one man has underestimated the generosity of the Creator in placing him where he is, only to find a multitude of unhappy divergences as he moves on to "greener" pastures. He then finds himself making his way back home, with a heavy heart and his tail between his legs.

FAMILY

As a man chooses to create, nurture, and support his family, so shall his very being be centered, gratified, loved, and satisfied.

The man that takes the substantial risk of having a family sets sail into uncharted waters that cannot be known in advance. It's driving without a map, compass, or any other navigational instrument. Yet, this is often where the greatest blessings lie, and there can be no other comparable experience in life to having a wife and children. The man that recognizes this embraces the unique opportunity to create new life and bring it to maturity finds a love and dedication coming back to him that he could not imagine beforehand. As he invests daily in the well being, development, and care of his family, his life expands exponentially and his sense of a greater world outside his previously limited focus is enormous. All the love and time invested then comes back, and there is closeness and loyalty that is rarely found outside a family unit. As this man ages and moves on, he finds that his life continues through his children and grandchildren, and he leaves behind a tangible remembrance of his very existence.

PLANNING

*A*s a man chooses his level of commitment to planning, so shall he experience a pleasing, relaxed, and reasonably predictable life.

While life is by nature uncertain, the man that has a thoughtful approach to the future encounters fewer bumps in the road than the one that does not. His vision for his future, coupled with a firm grasp on his own personal realities and that of his family, are the very building blocks for a fulfilling life and dreams that really do come true. Should he couple his well-developed sense of planning to an action plan that he is committed to, he all but assures a favorable outcome in most areas.

Sadly, most men bolt through life in a rapid, haphazard, and unpredictable manner. Living moment-to-moment and day-to-day, the future is of little or no concern. This man has a "live for today" attitude and either cannot or will not plan for his future or his family's. He overplays his hand in most venues [eating, drinking, spending, and indulging] then wonders why he struggles with the unexpected events that happen to everyone. Like a boat already off course and headed for the rocks, his life is then swamped with the choppy action of unexpected weather fronts coming through. In a way, this man suffers from overconfidence, delusions of grandeur, and is prone to fantasy. He is the boat captain that never checks the weather before departing, fails to top off the gas tank, and leaves his maps at home. It's just a matter of time before he ends up stranded or wrecked on a reef that he did not see. In a further sad and unfortunate way, this man then blames anyone he can find for his condition, including his Creator, and considers his well-thought-out and carefully planned counterpart to be lucky, undeserving, and neglectful of his condition. When enough of these men that fail to plan and employ a disciplined approach band together, we have a country that seeks to rebalance the well-earned results of the planner in an unfair way.

It's called socialism.

ORGANIZATION

As a man chooses and dedicates himself to organiza-tion, so shall he find order, peace, harmony, power, and efficiency in all his daily duties, responsibilities and callings.

Like a well-tuned engine that requires little to get it going and easily hits its optimum speed, the orga-nized man jumpstarts his life and zips along without the drag of trying to locate the necessary tools needed to do the job at hand. His every inspiration, effort, and thought is fully translated into productivity without delay or derailment. His natural inherent horsepower is reached and maintained quickly, easily, and steadily.

The man that shuns organization or cannot bring himself to invest a portion of each day organizing his life is a prime candidate for frustration, failure, and inef-ficiency. He may well be talented, and like his well-or-ganized counterpart, have a high-powered engine as his gift from his Creator. However, this engine takes forever to get started, hesitates, fails, needs constant maintenance, and probably never ever hits top speed. His lack of organization dooms him to a life of mediocrity, uncertainty, and inconsistency.

TECHNOLOGY

As a man chooses his level of commitment to technology, so shall his relative advantage and efficiency be in all his endeavors.

Like a supercharger on a racecar, the man's speed and efficiency are multiplied up in a dramatic manner, separating him from his competitors. A man that matches the latest, most powerful technology to his lifestyle, plan, and purpose finds he is one step ahead of his already ambitious goals without the back-breaking strain and anguish that usually accompanies life's chores and duties. If this same man takes the time to fully understand that technology and receive the proper training and advice, he grabs a foothold or a position in life that is hard to dislodge. This technology acts like a well-fortified castle, creating a barrier between him and those that would do him harm. In fact, life's circumstances can change markedly and still this man's life proceeds with some continuity.

A man that cannot be bothered with technology, sees it as evil, or unworthy of his time and attention, leaves himself wide open to obsolescence, inefficiency, and eventual failure. This man incorrectly perceives technology as just a bunch of tricks, or just another tool in the toolbox of life, nothing special. He then finds himself behind the eight ball in mostly every task-driven aspect of his life, and falling further and further behind. Should this same man happen to be middle-aged or older, he quickly loses his ability to relate to — or communicate with — the up and coming set that has moved into key positions of authority and influence. This man starts to resemble an image of something near by, but grows dimmer and dimmer as one moves further and further away until this man is no longer visible to life's key connections, opportunities, spontaneous moments, and get-togethers. He's literally an afterthought, if even that.

Place of Worship

*A*s a man chooses his place of worship and devo-
tion to his Creator, so shall his sense of sanity and
cosmic understanding be developed and reinforced.

The range, breadth, and width of choice is indeed
both impressive and imposing. Even within the same
general religion or belief structure there will be defin-
able and sometimes divergent differences from church
to church. So man's choice here is crucial as his atti-
tudes, beliefs, and inherent understanding of good and
evil will be molded and shaped. A man that understands his need for spiritual guidance and commits to
finding a church that will enhance his life and personal
development while offering opportunities to serve and
be served in his community, acquires a vital link to God
and mankind that simply cannot be acquired on his
own. The very act of worship, praise, and thanksgiving
reinforces his sense of the Creator's goodness, kindness, and love for his creation. The resulting stability,

peace, goodwill, and generosity that follows is like a refreshing spring that offers living water.

The man that cannot be bothered with church is at great risk of developing a strange and perverted self-made set of beliefs. Isolated, alone and without access to the concentrated understanding and focus that a dedicated and well-educated church leader brings, he is left stymied in his understanding of life. He is likely to have shifting values, unbalanced and unhealthy priorities, and a self-focus and self-absorption that creates a small circle of life indeed. After enough years on his own, this man is at risk of developing an arrogance and hardness of heart that only extreme adversity can puncture. More often than not, this man becomes increasingly disconnected from God and his fellow man. He has relied on his own inherent goodness, strength, and wisdom and that well eventually runs dry without being refreshed in a community of believers and worshipers.

PERSONAL MEDICINE AND HEALTHCARE

Man, by nature, is easily led and follows others in authority like sheep. Most everything he hears from recognized authorities becomes fact, and there is little testing of the validity of what he hears or what the experts tell him to do. Since a man's health and well being are of paramount importance to him, he should be aware of the impact of his decision to trust his health to any doctor or institution that pretends to know what is best. Sadly, he is often *deluded* and *misinformed* on just how effective and capable his healthcare choice has performed and is performing right now. More often than not, the repercussions — both direct and indirect — of modern traditional medicine are at best uncomfortable and at worst fatal.

This man must be a direct descendant of the passengers on the ill-fated Titanic of many years ago. Passengers on the Titanic were assured that it was, for all practical purposes, unsinkable. It was, after all, the greatest modern marvel of engineering ever made, and so there was no need to be in any way concerned. Just completely trust and be assured of your safety. In the end, when the Titanic struck a huge, mostly hidden iceberg, the damage was so great and the end came so swiftly that there was no time to get the required assistance. A great number were lost and not one even suspected that he was doomed the minute they stepped foot on the boat and trusted the Titanic crew for their safety and welfare. So it is with the man that has completely put his faith in the wrong healthcare system, he never sees it coming, and when he does, it's too late.

As a man chooses his personal medicine and healthcare, so shall his very time on earth be enhanced or reduced, and his quality of life be determined.

A wise man that understands nature, his body, and the need to work in harmony with God's creation will gravitate toward a holistic approach. His choice of a *naturopathic* option confirms this, leaving the masses to flood the traditional doctors' offices and hospitals with their incessant demands and problems of which there are often no lasting answers. Sure, the road traveled may be a bit slower making fundamental life changes and changing your diet requires a lot more effort and discipline than popping the latest pill the pharmaceutical companies are pushing. However, the results are often just as effective and without destructive side effects. This man takes responsibility for his health, sees it as a lifestyle issue, and makes the necessary adjustments. He reaps a double benefit, a longer life, and a more harmonious and stress-reduced lifestyle even as his impatient, lazy, trusting counterparts are taken away and laid to rest before their time.

ATTITUDE

A s a man chooses his attitude and focus, so shall the entire course of his life unfold and be experienced.

This attitude is no more than a *settled way of thinking* that has now solidified and become the very character of his soul and spirit. This character becomes the defining element in most every situation and relationship, with the corresponding results playing out exactly as they should for the man's mindset.

A man that chooses to take responsibility for his thoughts, feelings, actions and words finds that he is continually learning and can thereby make rapid adjustments when he is out of sync with reality. If he has devoted himself to some steady spiritual study, so much the better. His full and complete understanding of the Creator's method and model then leaves him with a vivid image and detailed instructions on where his energy and focus should be. If this same man also had wise and upright parents, mentors, and community and business leaders, he automatically knows what his mindset should be as he passes through the various stages of life. He has feelings but is not run by them. His focus is broad and wide and he cares for his neighbor as he cares for himself. His attitude is such that he brings blessings to all that know him.

The man that chooses to abdicate responsibility for himself, others and life in general quickly finds himself sinking into a miry pit of despair, disillusionment, anxiety, recklessness, and apathy. He nearly always sees himself as the victim, or looks at others as potential victims to be fleeced, used, and abused. He has no use for spiritual things, is totally self-centered and without understanding, wisdom, or grace. His emotions and feelings run him and his life represents a series of train wrecks, for himself and most of his close associations. He is indiscriminate, stupid, and unwilling to learn or receive correction. More often than not, he ends up alone, sick, broke, and quite possibly in and out of prison. Should he be brilliant and adept at manipulating and controlling others, he rots on the inside and eventually implodes into his own personal hell.

INTUITION AND INSTINCT

D ay in and day out, every man is faced with important decisions that require a wise and thoughtful response. Yet, analysis and study do not always yield the right answer or course of action. Often, only accessing and relying on one's intuition and instinct can find the correct pathway.

The man that chooses to stay plugged into his *subconscious mind* and acts accordingly will travel an entirely different pathway than those that do not. He understands the reflective and meditative process and will trust his lifeline to the Creator to take him in the right direction. When in doubt, he asks for help, attempts to go deeper, and holds off until it feels right. Listening to the still small voice within, he puts his ego and pride aside and trusts his instincts to take him in the right direction. What this man knows is that there are small, indefinable, and sometimes infinitesimal clues that his situation is feeding back to him, even if they cannot be initially identified by the conscious and rational mind. When faced with what appears to be a glorious opportunity to all around him, he sometimes backs away at the last minute because it does not feel right. When pressed for a reason for his decision, he cannot, and is often at a loss for words. More often than not, he turns out be right and those around him suddenly see him as a genius that can see around corners. His life then continues onward and upward, with no destructive departures from his plan or purpose.

Another man, also intelligent, smart and thoughtful, relies exclusively on rational thought and analysis. He determines a course of action, sets his mind, and goes forward. Along the way to his objectives, he finds a number of interesting and compelling options to his original plan but immediately discounts them as unworthy of his time and attention. After all, he knows where he is going and these simply represent unneeded distractions and are not what he had in mind as he runs life's course. This man is not too different than a man that is determined to find gold, but along the way finds compelling mining options for silver or even diamonds. He bypasses what the Creator has dropped into his lap and chooses to go forward doggedly, determined to find gold. His instincts have totally malfunctioned and maybe he passes up the opportunity of lifetime with his single-minded pursuit of his goals.

The Cumulative Effect
(of all choices)

A man that has no understanding of choice tends to see his station in life at any one point in time as being a unique, temporary, or one time event. He often finds himself in a precarious or undesirable position and it feels like bad luck or even a freak or unusual situation. It feels like the world is against him and he feels persecuted, isolated, and alone in his misery. This leads to dwelling on his undesirable and sometimes pathetic situation and there is little to no critical self-examination, just a whirlwind of hate, anger, bitterness, and depression at the outside forces he sees as his enemy.

More often than not, this man has been making indulgent, destructive, and selfish choices for many years, possibly even decades. These decisions have become so ingrained — so much a part of his daily life — that they start to merge together, and there is a shrinking awareness of the corrosive effect on his life.

His life can be likened to a new car that starts out in great condition and with the potential to go one hundred, two hundred, or even three hundred thousand miles with minimal interruption and maximum performance. Requiring only a steady hand, protective garaging and regular service to be a reliable and enjoyable mode of transportation.

However,this man totally takes his brand new shiny vehicle for granted. He drives too fast, while drinking, or ignores unsafe conditions, and pushes the limit of his car's abilities. When the car ends up wrapped around a telephone pole, he curses his luck and blames everyone and everything but himself. On closer inspection, one finds that the brakes were worn, the tires were shot, and the car was so filthy that a clear view of the road was nigh impossible. Proper maintenance and respect for the car were almost totally absent, and what looked like a one time, even freak accident, was really a matter of long-term neglect, disrespect, and indifference. *The cumulative effect of his choices was funneling him toward*

an inevitable destiny, and there was precious little anyone or
anything could do to derail the freight train of poor choices
over a great many years. Once his life totally collapses, he
now has a daunting task, if he chooses to go forward.
A slow, painful, and lengthy period of self-examination, review and reconstruction. Each and every aspect
of his life needs to be reconsidered, rethought and the
appropriate changes made. It's a long and arduous
process, and it takes great commitment and determi-
nation to start over, almost from scratch.

Once again, if we look at this man's life as the previously hereto mentioned vehicle, it's in effect, a total
rebuild. Like a dirty old car, left to rot in a barn for
thirty or forty years, there is practically nothing that
will not need to be replaced, repaired, or reengineered.
Yet even at this debauched, broken down and disrespected state, there is hope. If someone, hopefully the
man himself, can see the potential to be great once
again, something magical happens. The vision of a
new life — a new state of being — energizes his efforts

and the former self is left behind as the new spirit-filled man emerges. Our broken down car, not worth anything (even as replacement parts), is gradually being transformed from the inside out. Sure, it takes time and great energy and expertise, but the result is all but certain when the commitment is made. Should the original owner of our "barn find" return two, three, or five years later, he finds such a transformation that he is not able to conceive that this is indeed the same vehicle. It's beyond anything he could possibly imagine, and this seemingly worthless pile of junk now shines with such vigor that others come from miles around just to get a look at it. It's what they call a classic car, restored to its original beauty and magnificence. Unable to contain his pride and joy at his stunning new possession, the owner now parades his car at classic car rallies and shows and drives it without hesitation all around town. So is the man that chooses to put his pride and ego totally aside and recommit to his life and purpose with everything he has, and allow his Creator to lead him to the people and resources that will be the cata-

lysts for his transformation.

The man that is fully and completely aware and cog-

nizant of the magnitude of his choices starts out life on an

entirely different path.

A bit meditative and thoughtful by nature, this man

has taken each important decision in his life as fully

worthy of study, analysis, and review. His choices are

heavily influenced by the goals and objectives he has

for life and they are generally high-minded and noble

pursuits. He may start out a bit off target here and there

but quickly recovers and seeks out the necessary guid-

ance to bring him back on track. There is wisdom in a

multitude of counselors and this man does not hesitate

to seek out the latest and greatest leaders in his com-

munity to advance his life. His pride does not get in his

way, but works for him as he recognizes the immense

value the Creator has placed in him and desires to ful-

fill his highest plan and purpose.

The net result of high-minded, noble, and progressive thinking are choices that emphasize the long-term over the short term. So his life looks a bit staid or even boring for a while compared to his flamboyant counterpart that lives exclusively for today. The situation changes markedly as the reflective man starts to experience the fruits of his labor and his superior choices. He can be compared to a small seedling or tree that is developing a strong and deep root system. On the surface, the small tree looks pretty insignificant, unimportant, and maybe even weak. As time goes by and the properly cared for tree grows, it becomes more and more stable and capable of sustaining additional life beyond itself. The will 'o the wisp bushes and plants are blown all over the place, but the developing tree is creating an underground root system that becomes life-sustaining and all but immovable. These underground roots, hundreds if not thousands, represent the *Cumulative Effect* of all his good choices. These roots not only create enormous stability, they are the vital link between the tree and it sources of nourishment and sustenance. The tree becomes a self-sustaining unit, and as it continues to grow and mature, it becomes more powerful and mighty in both stature and significance.

In the end, the man that makes wise choices has a blessed life so far and away superior to his thought-less counterpart that it seems utterly unfair, sad, and maybe even cruel. In reality, nothing could be further from the truth. Each man came to reap what he sowed, more than he sowed, and in a whirlwind. The multipli-cation effect of his choices ends up with either a posi-tive or negative compounding of the results. There are no small choices — they all count — and everything either contributes or subtracts from his life.

As A Man Chooses, So Shall His Life Be.

CPSIA information can be obtained at www.ICGtesting.com
Printed in the USA
BVOW07s0414211114

376061BV00001B/8/P